STRINGSTASTIC
Level 2
DOUBLE BASS

By Lorraine Chai

USA Edition

STRINGSTASTIC

PO BOX 815 Epping NSW 1710 Australia
www.stringstastic.com
Copyright © 2023 Lorraine Chai

Book design by Meilisa Lengkong

All rights reserved.
Reproduction in whole or in part for any use whatsoever is strictly prohibited.

THE AUTHOR
LORRAINE CHAI

Lorraine is a multi-talented instrumentalist, international educator, and world-class coach. She graduated from the Sydney Conservatorium of Music with a Bachelor of Music Studies in 2008 and completed her Graduate Diploma of Education at the Australian Catholic University a year later. Lorraine also holds a Postgraduate Diploma in Education from Birmingham City University.

Having grown up in a musical family, Lorraine began piano lessons at the age of four and violin at the age of six, giving her first violin performance at just seven years of age. Lorraine started teaching violin at the age of 14 and founded a string ensemble at her local church. From there, teaching and performing became her passion.

Lorraine loves finding new and exciting ways students can learn their instrument in a classroom setting as well as in private lessons. Along with her musical journey and exposure to the various educational methods including Kodaly, Suzuki, Orff, and Dalcroze, Lorraine has also attended Alexander Technique workshops and has found that she can integrate these various methods into her own teaching technique for the benefit of her students.

Lorraine has an extensive ensemble and orchestral experience in Malaysia and Australia. Lorraine is currently the Music Director of Stringstastic Pty Ltd and is an active member of the Australian Strings Association, AUSTA NSW. She also co-ordinates instrumental programmes and runs string ensembles for some of Sydney's most celebrated schools.

PREFACE

Stringstastic double bass Level 2 builds on the knowledge that young players have gained in Stringstastic double bass Level 1. Stringstastic double bass Level 2 extends that knowledge through games and fun graphics to assist young beginner double bassists to help them better understand the instrument and to learn music theory in an enjoyable way.

This Stringstastic series can be used in a private lesson or alongside the violin, viola, and cello book series in a classroom setting.

For extra resources, go to www.stringstastic.com to download them for free.

Have fun!!

ACKNOWLEDGEMENT

This book was made possible with the encouragement of my family and loved ones. I would like to thank the following for their advice and input in making this book possible.

Dr. Rita Crews OAM, FMusA (honoris causa), PhD(UNE), BA(Hons), AMusTCL, FMusicolASMC, GradCertDistEd (UNE), HonFNMSM, DipMus (honoris causa) (AICM) MIMT, MACE, MMTA, JP.

Dr. Anthony Clarke DMA, MMus, Grad Dip, BMus Ed, DSCM, FTCL, LMusA, AMusA

Prof Barry Green BMus, MMus, renowned double bassist and educator, former executive director of ISB, author of 3 double bass method books

Dr. h.c. Claus A. Freudenstein is an International double bass soloist and educator, founder of Freudenstein-Minibass and "The Bassmonsters", Artistic Director of "The Bavarian Bassdays", author

CONTENTS

- **4**   REVISION
- **6**   TEMPO
- **8**   EIGHTH NOTE AND REST
- **10**   DYNAMICS
- **12**   2ND FINGER
- **14**   SLUR VS. TIE
- **16**   WHAT HAVE WE LEARNED SO FAR?
- **19**   NOTE MOVEMENT
- **21**   SHIFTING VS. PIVOTING
- **24**   WHOLE STEP AND HALF STEP
- **29**   REVISION - NOTE READING ON ALL STRINGS
- **31**   SCALES AND ARPEGGIOS
- **38**   KEY SIGNATURE VS. ACCIDENTAL
- **40**   ARTICULATION
- **42**   SIGNS
- **44**   LAST REVISION
- **47**   TEST

STRINGSTASTIC

Revision

1. Name the 4 open strings of the double bass.

   _____

   _____

   _____

   _____

2. Fill in the blanks.

NOTE	NOTE NAME	REST	REST NAME	VALUE
♩			Quarter rest	
		▬		2
	Whole note			4

3. Using whole notes, draw and name the notes of each string of the double bass. (Don't forget the #s).

E String

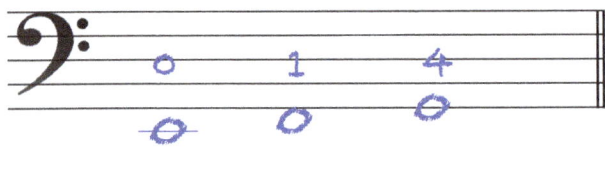

E   F#   G#

D String

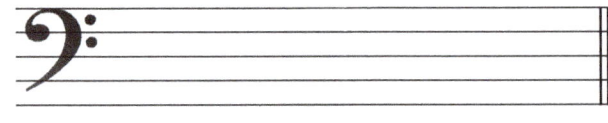

A String

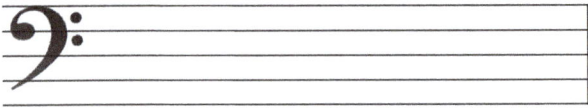

G String

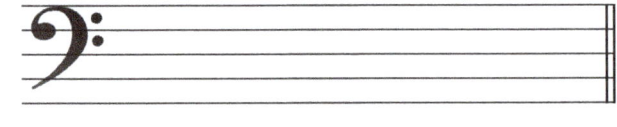

4. Put in the bar lines and write in the beats.

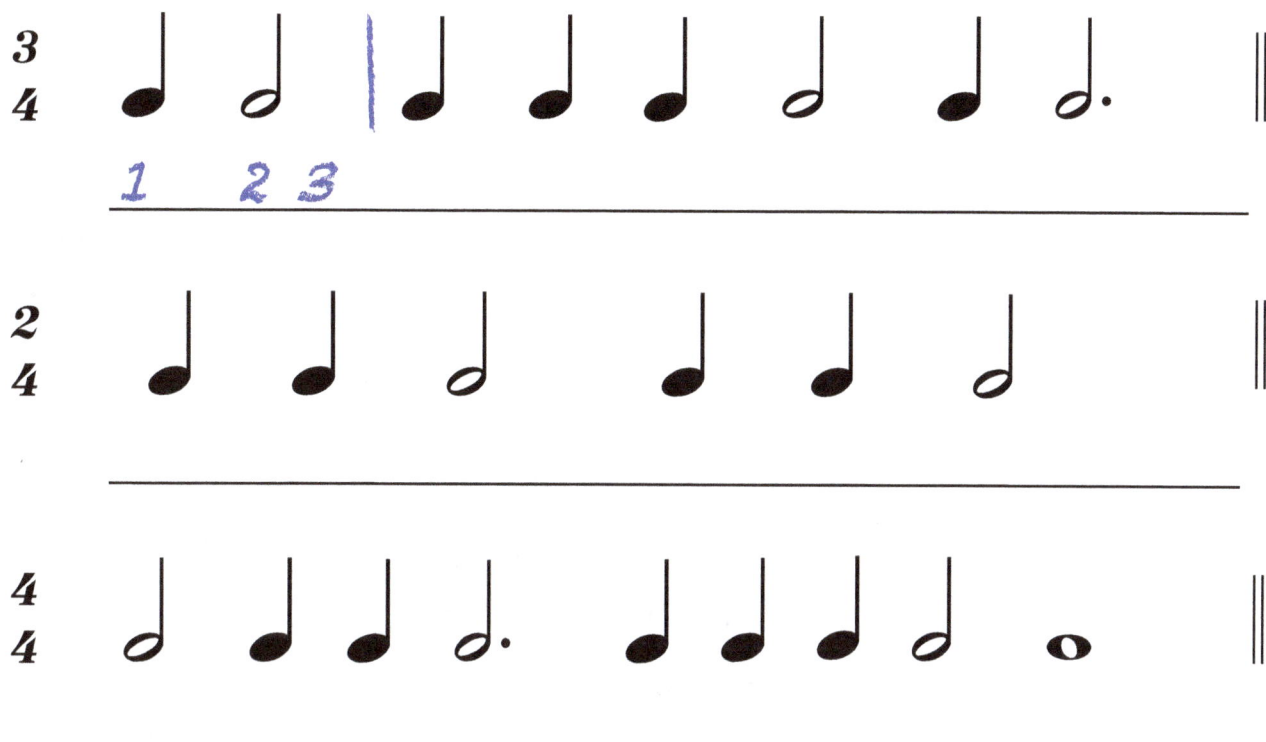

5. Name the missing notes of these fingerings on the fingerboard.

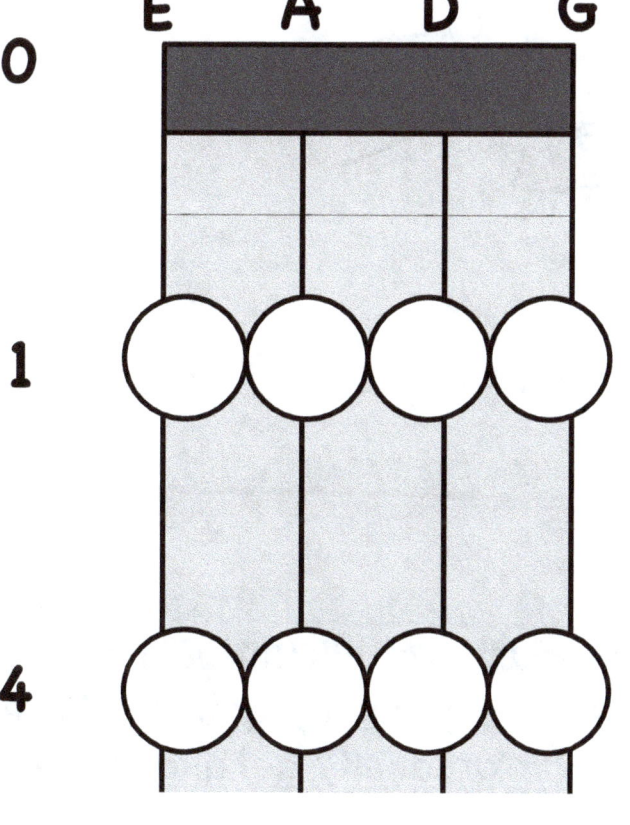

Tempo

Tempo is the speed at which music is played.

- fast — Allegro
- moderate speed — Moderato
- walking speed — Andante
- slowly — Adagio

accelerando (accel.) – gradually getting faster
rallentando (rall.) – gradually getting slower
ritardando (rit.) – gradually getting slower
a tempo – return to original speed

Match each picture to its meaning.

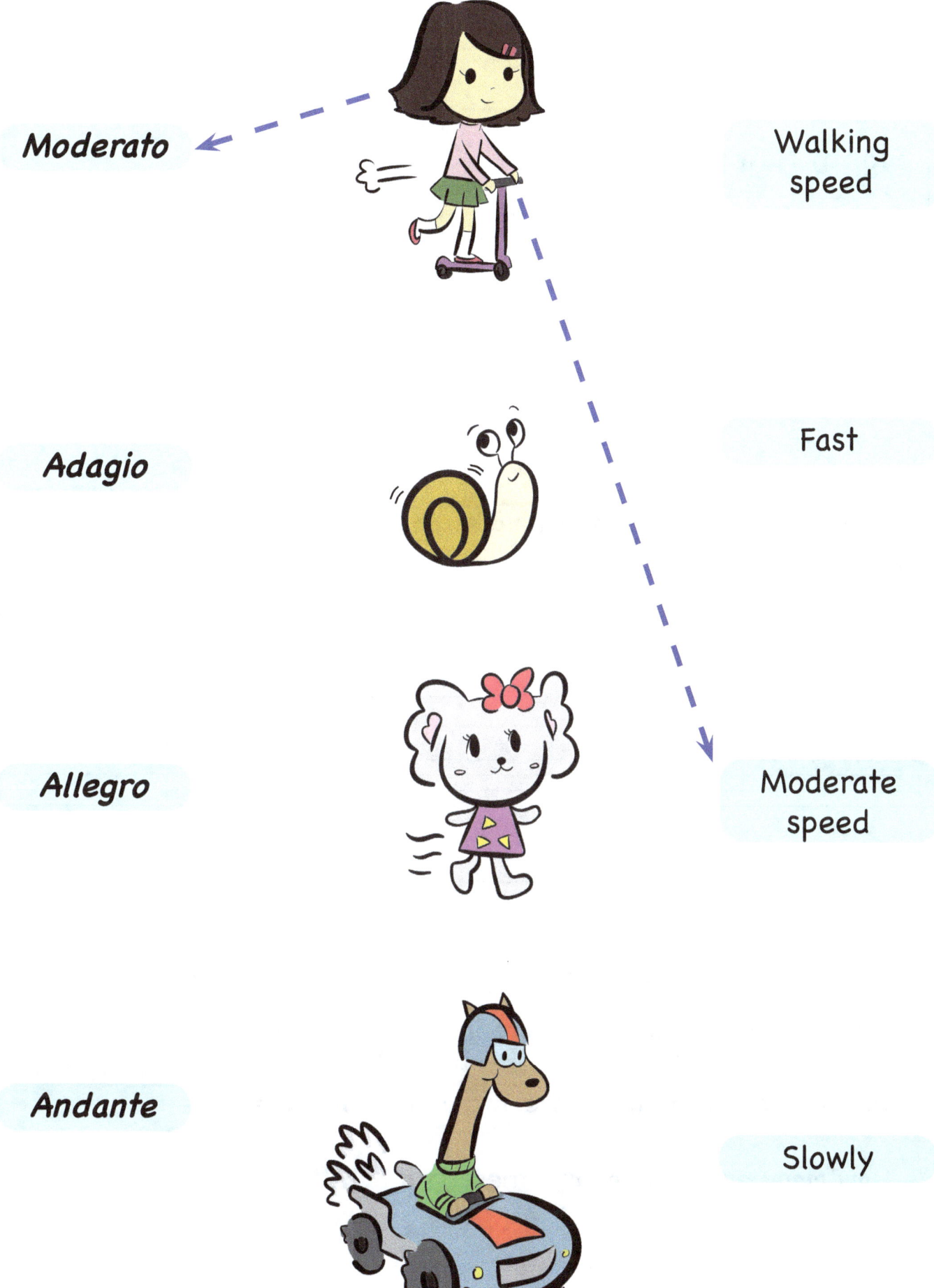

Quaver Note and Rest

NAME	NOTE	REST	VALUE
Eighth Note	♪ ←tail	tail→ 𝄾	½
2 Eighth Notes Joined	♫ ←beam = ♩		½ + ½ = 1

1. First, draw the note head (seed)
2. Draw the stem (stem of plant)
3. Last, draw the tail(s) or beam(s) (leaf)

Draw the tail for each of these notes and rests and write its value.

½

½

Answer the questions below.

1. How many half notes are there in a whole note?

2. How many quarter notes are there in a half note?

3. How many eighth notes are there in a half note?

4. A 𝅝 is equal to   ♪ s

5. A 𝄻 is equal to   𝄾 s

Tommy forgot to close the cover to his collection of bugs and now they are all over the living room. He has to get them back into their appropriate boxes before his mother comes home. Color the bugs according to the number of counts.

COUNTS	COLOUR
1	RED
2	BLUE
3	GREEN
4	YELLOW

How many bugs are there in the following?

Red   —   bugs

Blue   —   bugs

Green —   bugs

Yellow —   bugs

Dynamics

Dynamics refers to the volume of a sound or note.
Which animal makes a LOUD or soft sound?

We use Italian terms to express dynamics. Below are the meanings of each Italian term.

forte (f) – LOUD
piano (p) – soft
crescendo (cresc.) – <u+0332> – gradually getting louder
decrescendo (decresc.) – <u+0332> – gradually getting softer
diminuendo (dim.) – gradually getting softer

mezzo (m) – moderately (medium)
mezzo piano (mp) – moderately (medium) soft
mezzo forte (mf) – moderately (medium) loud

Fill in the blank below arranging each dynamic starting from the softest to the loudest.

_____ < *mp* < _____ < *f*

On the previous page, mark out the volume each animal makes by using *p* for *piano* or *f* for *forte*.

Guess what?

Play similar notes in a row on your double bass using different dynamics each time. (*f*, *p*, *cresc.*, *dim.*).

You can play this game with your friends. Ask them if they can guess what kind of dynamic you are playing.

2nd Finger

Let us revise the accidentals and our notes on the double bass following where the fingering strips are placed.

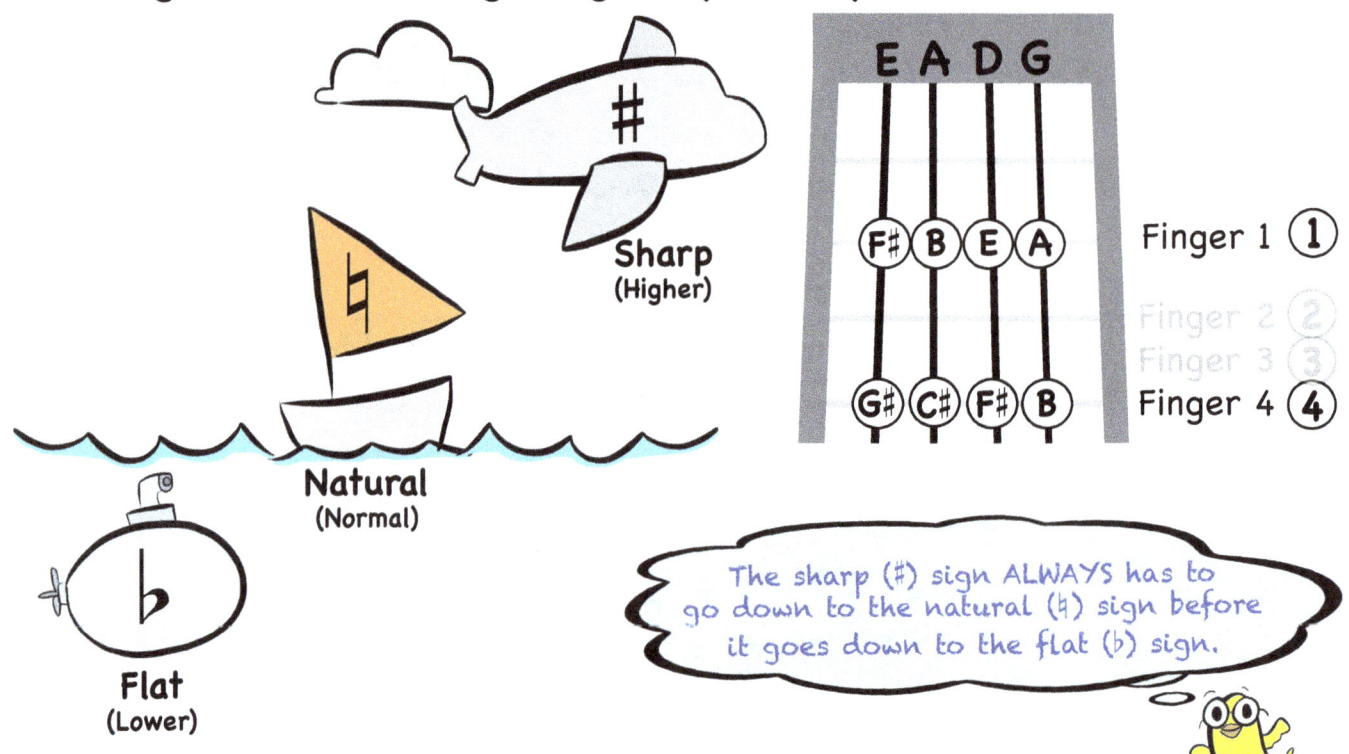

The pitch of the letter note is lowered when we use the 2nd finger instead of the 3rd or 4th finger.

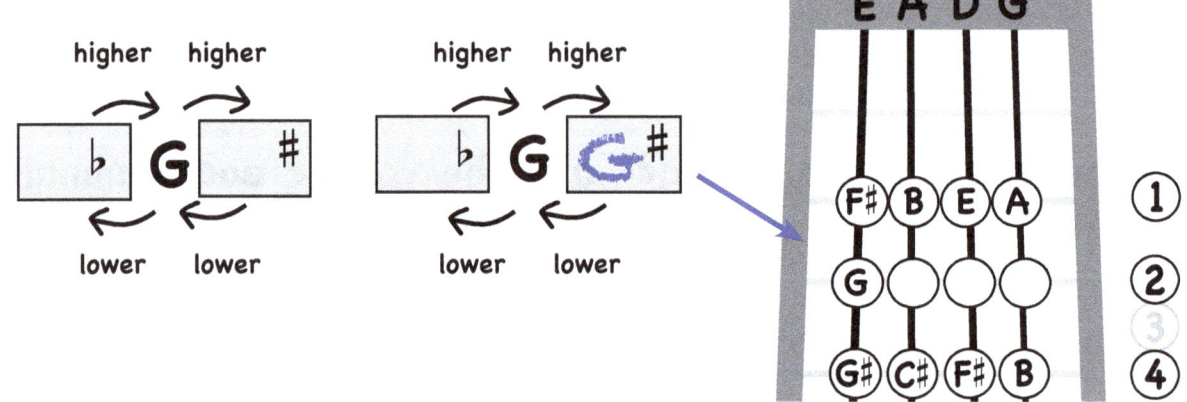

Name the notes below accordingly.

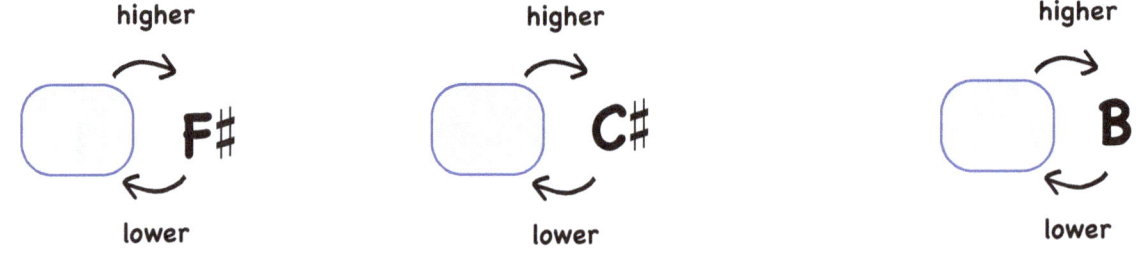

Lower each note and name them.

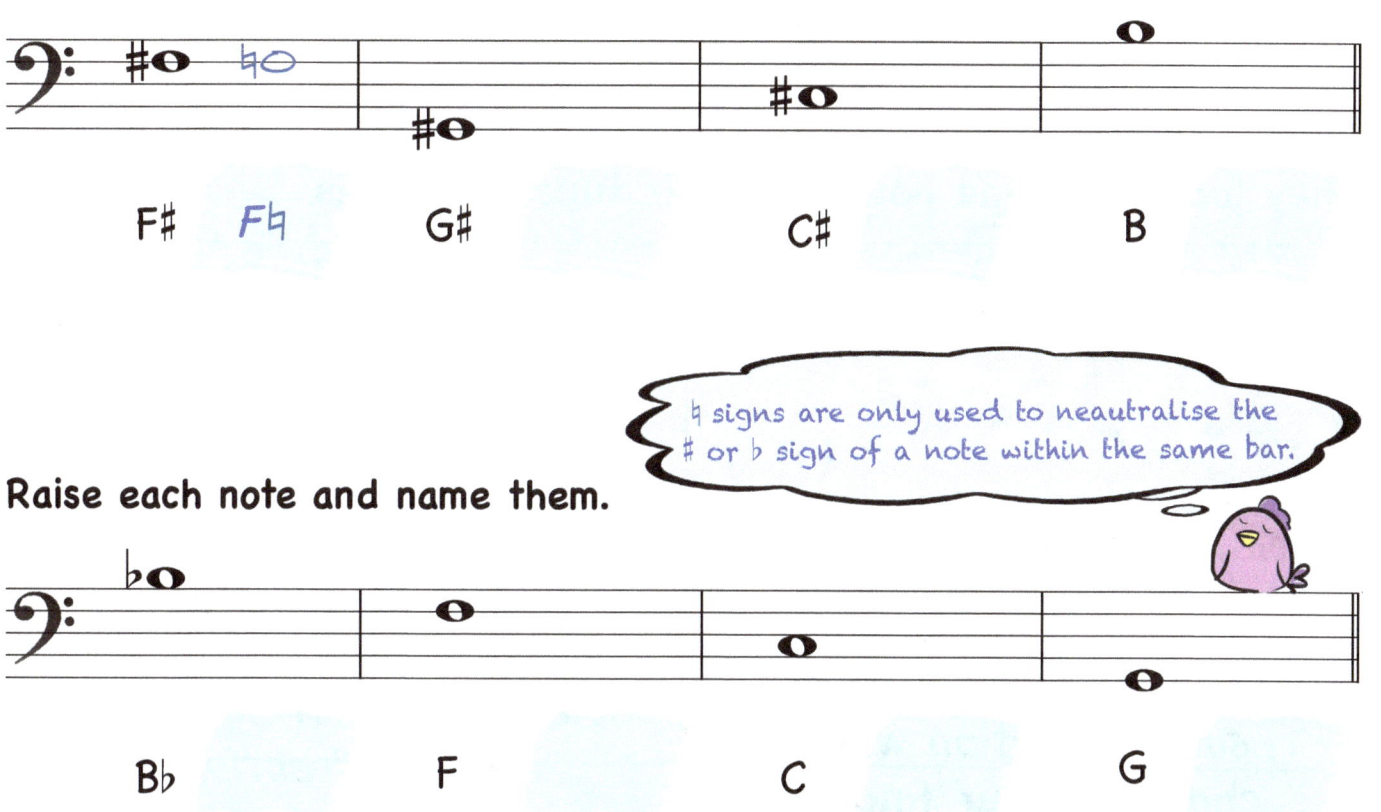

Raise each note and name them.

♮ signs are only used to neautralise the # or ♭ sign of a note within the same bar.

Draw the notes below as indicated. (Remember your ♮.)

Now add the number 2 on top of the notes that require the use of the 2nd finger.

Slur vs. Tie

Slurs and ties are curved lines joining 2 or more notes. They look the same however their function varies.

SLUR	TIE
← slur	← tie
Notes sound and played *smoothly*	*Hold* the note at the total amount of notes
Keep bow moving in the same direction while changing your fingers	Keep bow moving in the same direction
Joined between *different* notes	Joined between 2 of the *same* notes

How long do you hold these tied notes for?

♩ ♩ = 1 + 1 = 2

𝅗𝅥 ♩ = =

♩ ♩ ♩ = =

♩ ♩. = =

𝅗𝅥 𝅗𝅥 = =

Information: The Italian term for playing smoothly is legato.

Identify if these curved lines are either a tie or slur.

slur

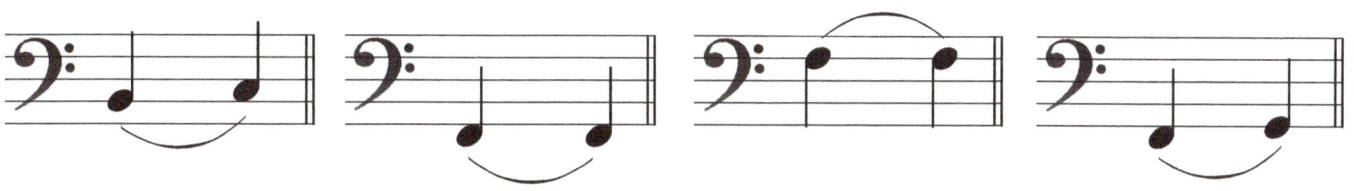

What have we learned so far?

What does "*Allegro*" mean?

What does "*Andante*" mean?

What does "*a tempo*" mean?

What is the total beats of all these rest and notes?

Fill in the blanks.

𝅗𝅥.	dotted minim	mp	
	gradually getting softer		LOUD
rit.		cresc.	
♪		𝄢 ♩ ♩ (slur)	slur
𝄢 ♩⌢♩			eighth rest
	half rest		gradually getting faster

Match each picture to its meaning.

Adagio   f

p   Allegro   accel.

Between 2 notes, circle one in which requires the use of the 2nd finger.

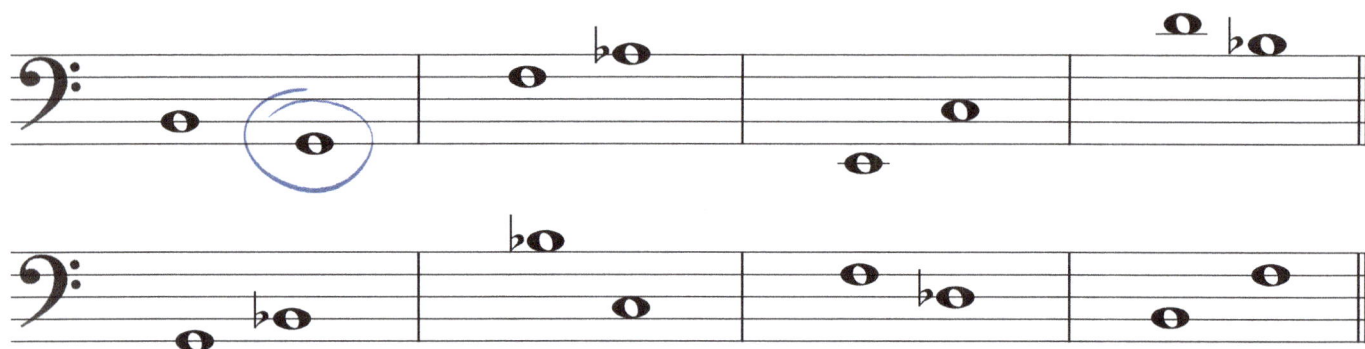

How many quarter beats are these notes and rests?

♩ = *1*   𝄽 =

♪ =   𝅗𝅥 =

𝅗𝅥. =   ▀ =

𝄾 =   ♫ =

▄ =   𝅝 =

Note Movement

Notice how notes move up or down in the stave. Be aware of how far the notes move (through a line or in a space).

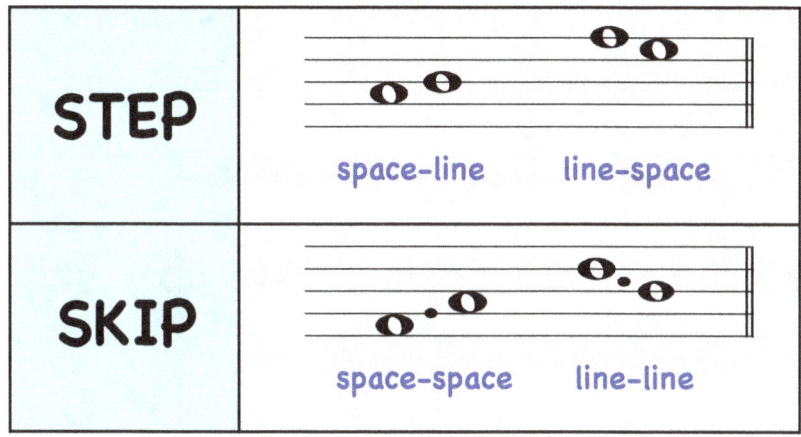

Circle the 2 notes moving by step.

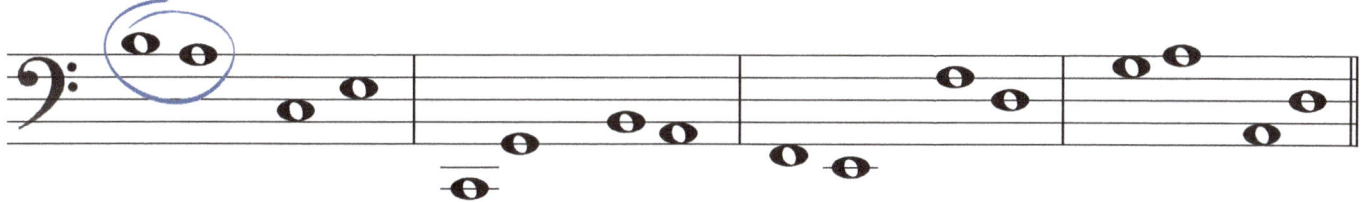

20
Where should these notes be?

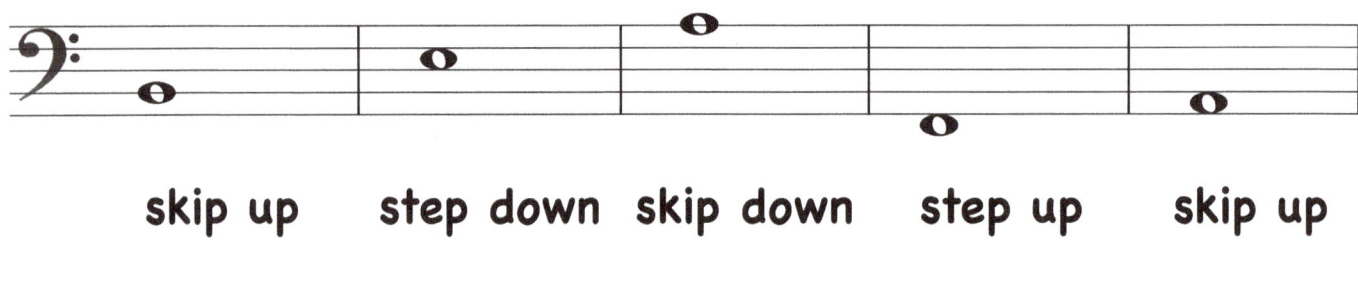

Name the movement of these notes.

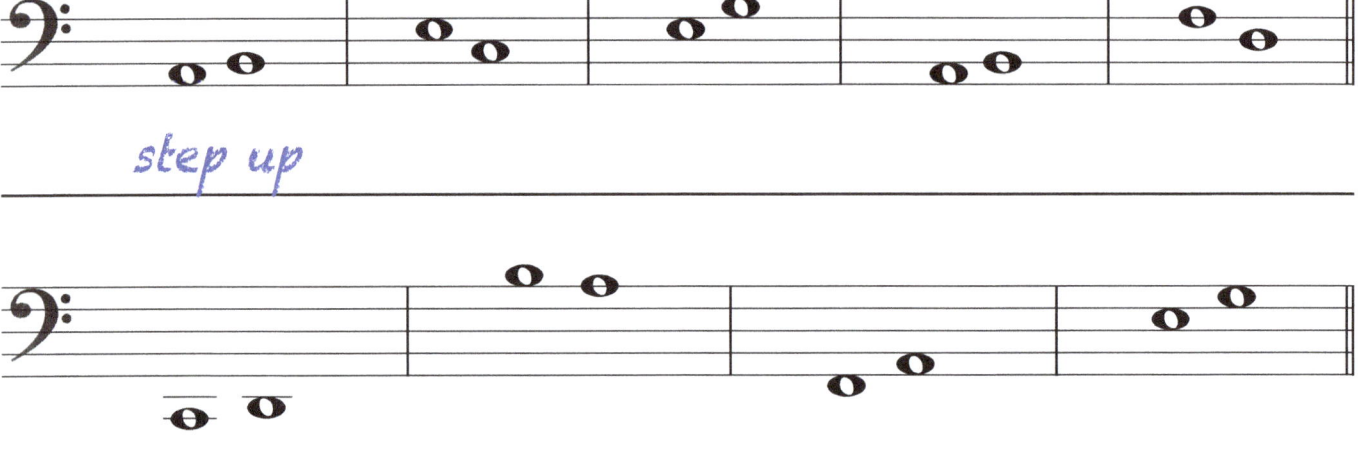

step up

Now add the fingering for all the notes on the questions above.

Shifting vs. Pivoting

Shifting and pivoting are techniques involving the left hand's movement on the fingerboard (like an escalator or hoverboard). When we first started learning the double bass, our hand position was close to the scroll.

Below is a table showing the difference between the two.

SHIFTING	PIVOTING
Left hand smoothly moves on the fingerboard.	
They do not have specific marking.	
Thumb moves with left hand (whole hand movement).	Thumb is <u>anchored</u> (rooted) while 1st finger stretching backwards.
Need to know where to move.	Easy to transition back to the original position
The thumb follows the movement of the whole arm.	*The left hand stretches or rocks over the thumb on the fingerboard.*

In the 1st and 2nd position, the hand can pivot forwards or backwards on the fingerboard. On the 3rd position, the hand can pivot further.

Take note that players may choose to learn 1 or both of these techniques. Watch our Virtual Theory Lessons on **www.stringstastic.com** to see the difference or get your double bass teacher to show you in your lesson.

Different positions

By now we should be 'experts' on the first position (original position shown in Level 1).

Double bass is a uniquely different instrument compared to the other string instruments as there are different ways of labelling the different positions as well as using half positions and the thumb position (the thumb is used on top of the fingerboard) **compared to the other string instruments.**

In order to identify the different positions depends on where the first finger is placed. If the first finger is moved to the 2nd strip on the fingering board, you are now in 2nd position. If the 1st finger is moved to the 3rd line, you are now in 3rd position and so on.

Shifting can be labelled with a dash (-) on top of the music notes on your music piece.

Benefits:
- gain more notes on each string
- more possibilities for fingerings to help play any tune
- help improve smooth playing of fast passages

Requirements:
- control of finger spacing (tone and semitone)
- standing fingertip position enabling smaller spacing
- elbow moves

One way is by using Roman Numerals to mark the different positions which is shown below,

    B♭ 1/2 Position
    B   I - First Position
    C   II - Second Position
    C♯ II 1/2 - Two 1/2 Position
    D   III - Third Position
    D♯ III 1/2 - Three 1/2 Position
    E   IV - Fourth Position
    F   V - Fifth Position
        etc.

With labeling using Roman Numerals, these TWO positions are the only positions we do not use on the double bass.

✗ 1 half position
✗ 4 half position

Some bass players do not use the different position as numbers but use patterns and the note name (letter name) of the position they shift to. Examples are shown as above in GREEN.

Try and play the notes below on each string using the different positions.

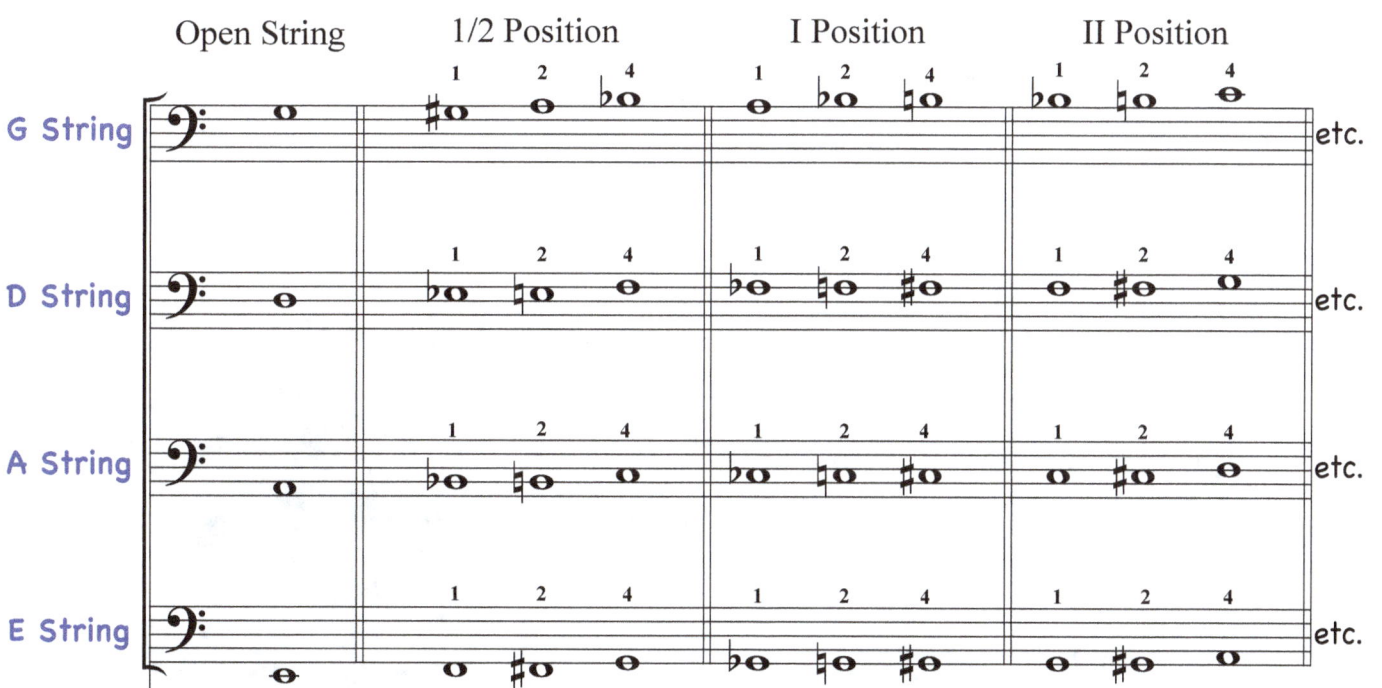

Printable for the complete exercise above is available at
www.stringstastic.com

Whole Step and Half Step

A <u>half step</u> is the smallest distance between 2 notes. When you play a half step on any part of the double bass, your notes would be <u>close to each other</u> on the fingerboard.

Let us revise our notes on the double bass on the original position.

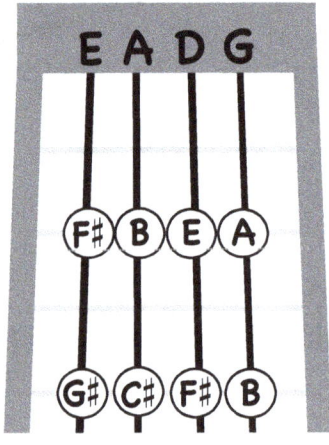

And a quick revision of your accidentals...

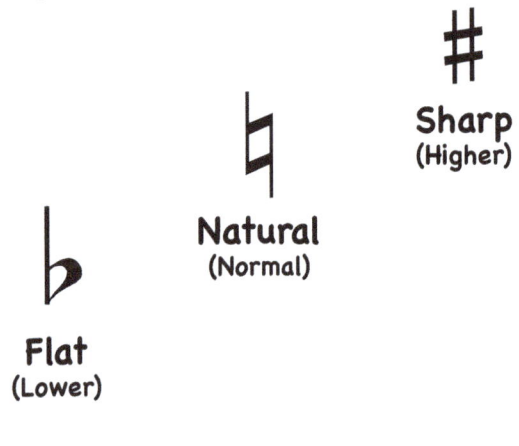

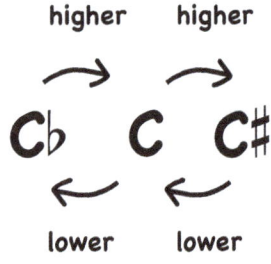

www.stringstastic.com

Insert the correct notes.

1.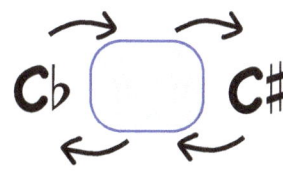

2.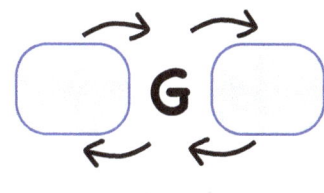

3.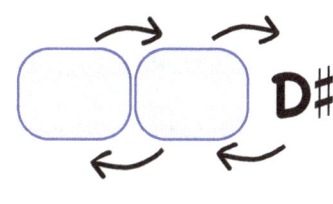

4.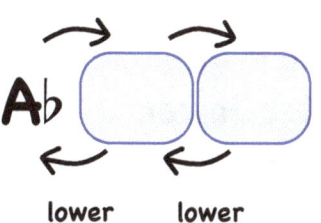

5.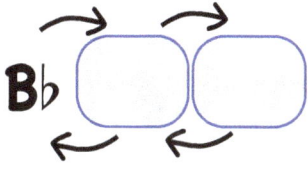

6.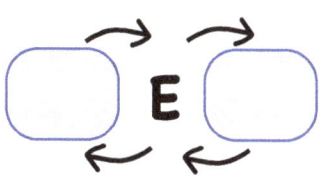

7.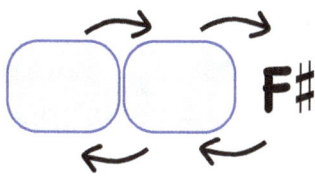

Let us look at the half step on the double bass fingerboard. You can see that we have included the 2nd finger notes here.
Circle 8 pairs of notes which are a half step apart.

Information: Enharmonic means TWO different note names that sound the same.

eg. E# = F

TIP: Name the first note and then visualize the notes on the fingerboard.

After each note, draw a note that is a half step higher.

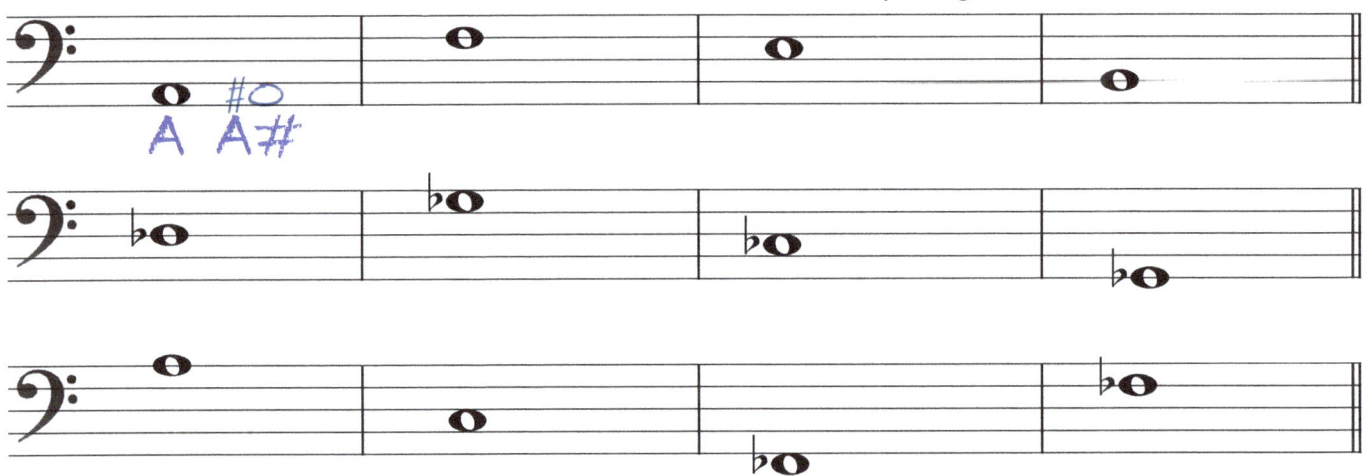

A   A#

After each note, draw a note that is a half step lower.

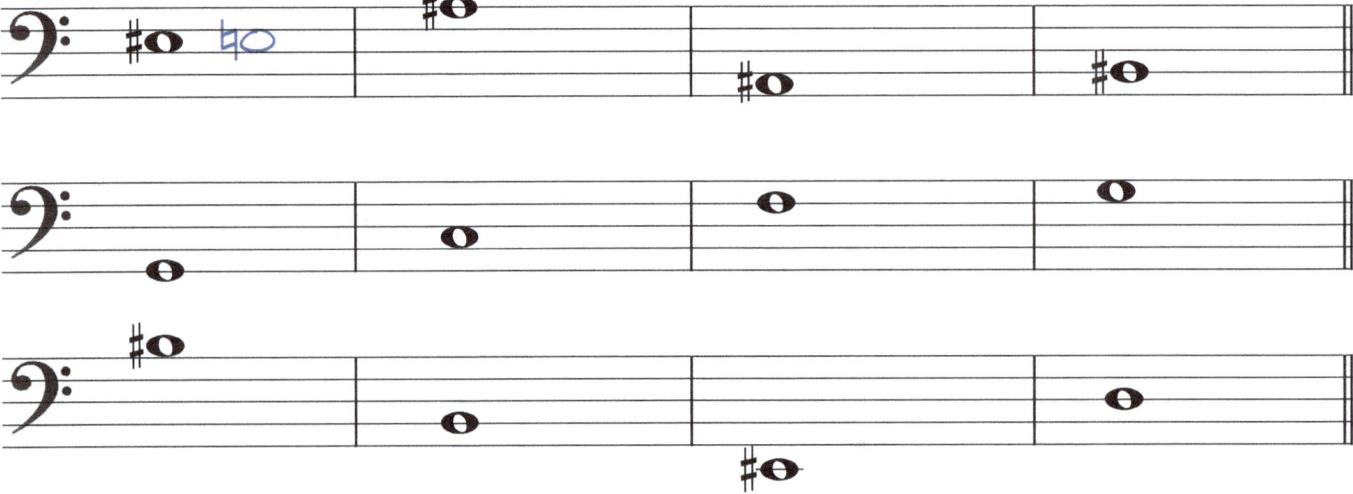

A **whole step** means the notes are 2 half steps away from each other.

When you play the double bass, the notes already has a **LARGE** space between them.

Circle 8 pairs of notes which are a whole step apart.

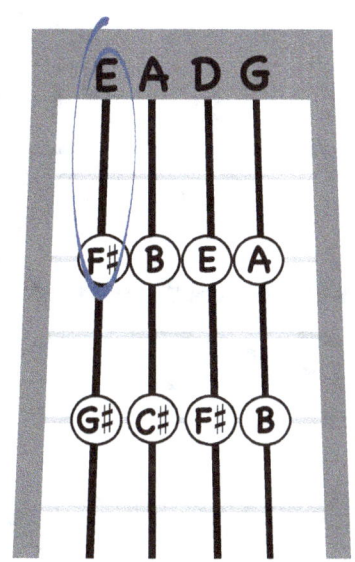

After each note, draw a note that is a whole step higher.

After each note, draw a note that is a whole step lower.

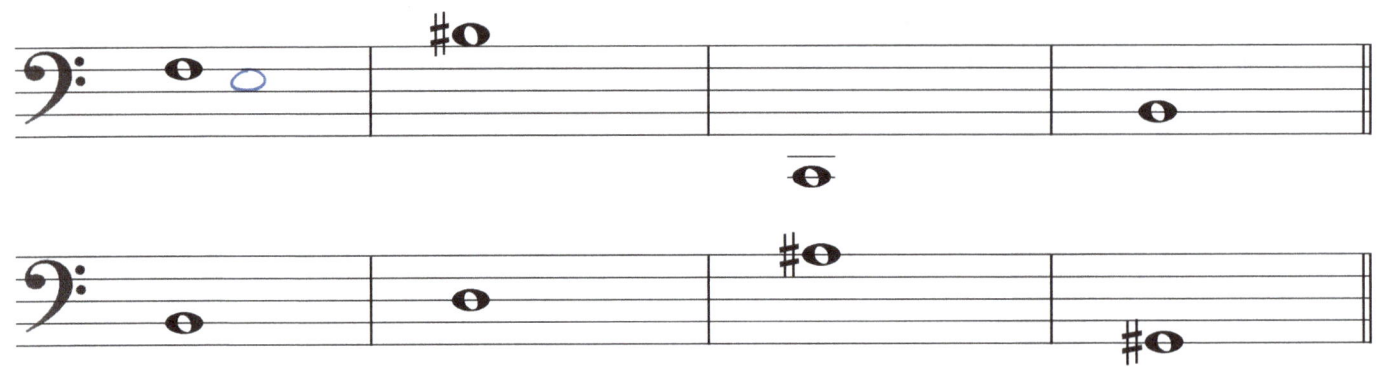

TIP: Name the first note and then visualize the notes on the fingerboard.

Draw the notes according to the steps.

| whole step up | half step up | half step down | whole step down |

| half step up | whole step up | whole step down | whole step up |

Revision (Note Reading on all Strings)

Using half notes, draw and name all the notes which can be played on each string. (Don't forget the #s.)

Careful of the stem directions

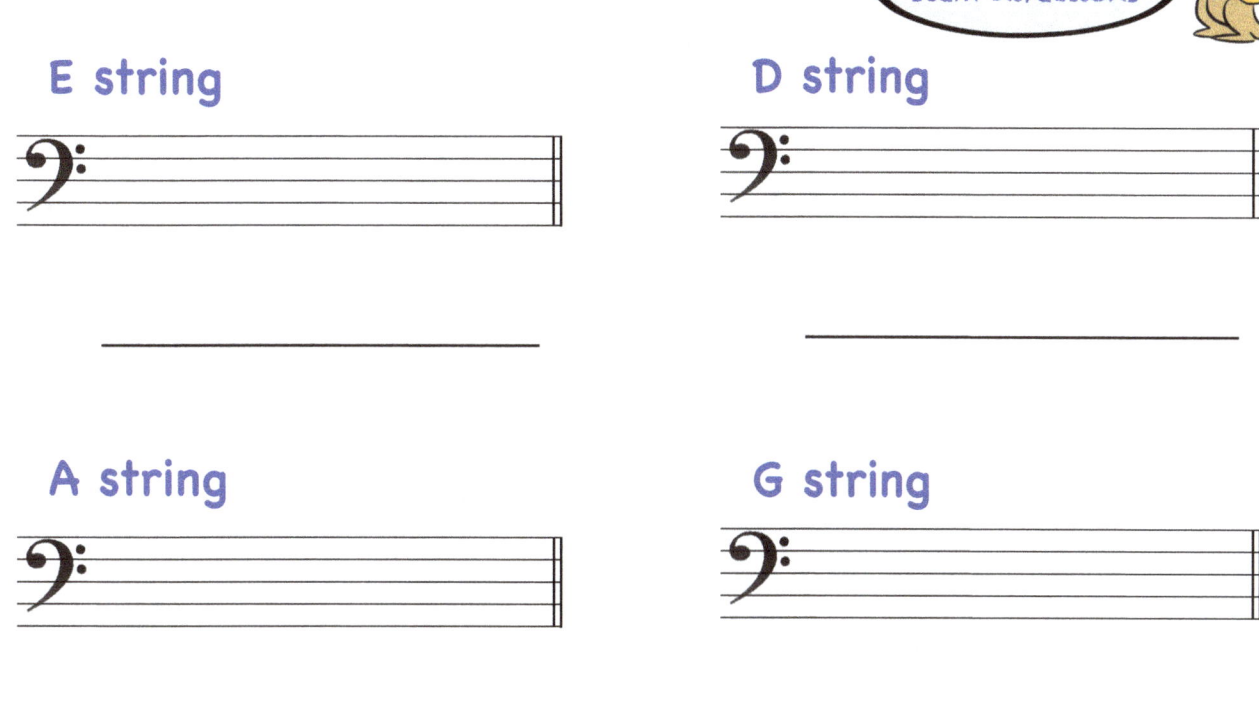

E string

D string

A string

G string

Name the notes.

G

Name the notes and put in the bar lines.

Match the notes below to the following words.

- BED 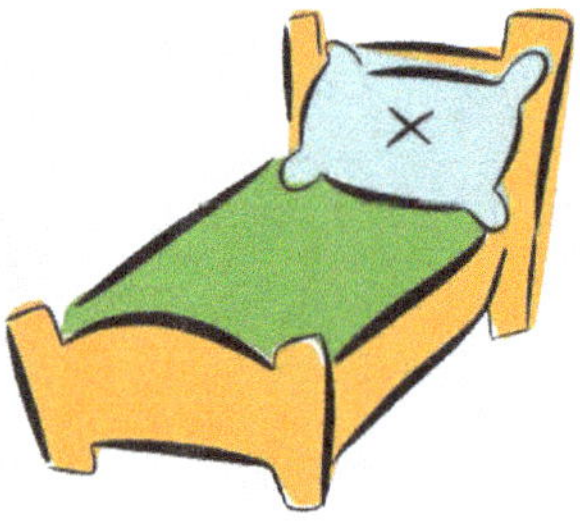 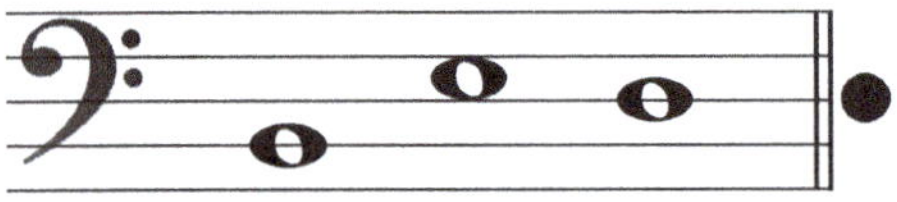
- BAG  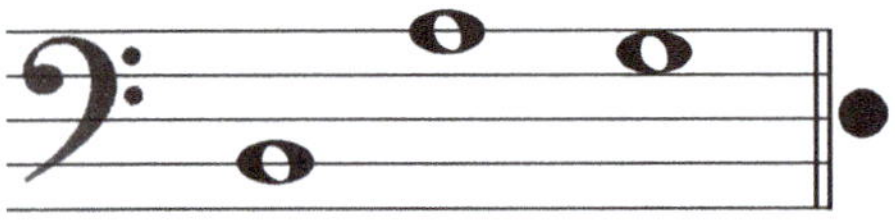
- FACE  
- CAGE

Scales and Arpeggios

A **Scale** is a musical ladder with notes stepping up and down in alphabetical order starting from the name of the note of the scale to the next note of the same name.

Eg.

C Major (1 octave)

C   D   E   F   G   A   B   C

Octave – is a series of 8 notes (example: A B C D E F G A).

It is the note and the same note higher or lower which includes all the notes in between.

What are the notes for these 2 scales?

G Major (1 octave)
- Remember to add a ♯ on the F as this scale has an F♯.

E Major (1 octave)
- Remember to add ♯s on the F and C notes as this scale has an F♯ and a C♯.

Let us start with the G major scale on the double bass.

G Major - G A B C D E F# G   (1 octave)

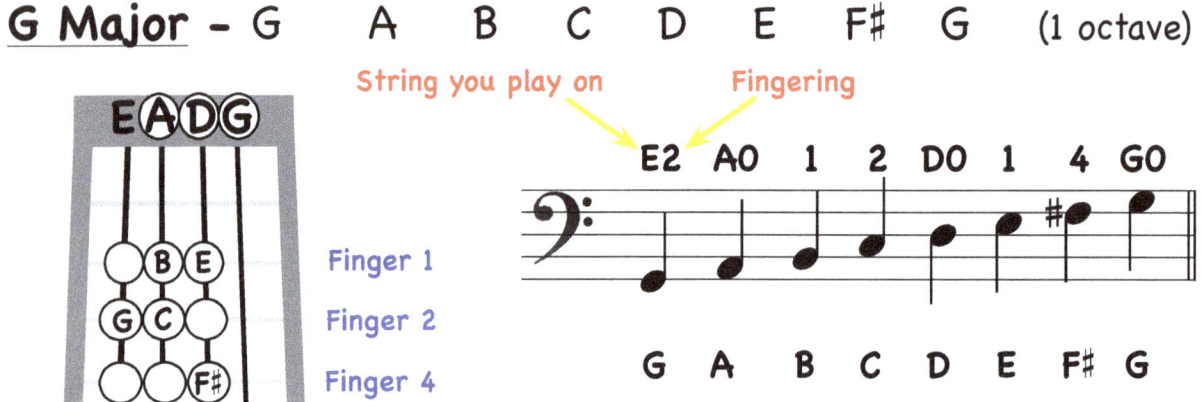

E Major - E F# G# A B C# D# E   (1 octave)

C Major - C D E F G A B C   (1 octave)

Try playing all these scales slowly on your double bass using the 2nd finger as well as shifting and pivoting where needed.
How did that go? Was it easy?

Now let us see if you can play these scales by memory. Could you play these scale by memory?

Did you remember to shift or pivot?

Write in the notes names on the fingerboard and using whole notes, draw the notes of these scales in an ascending (going up) order only for the G major scale.

G major (1 octave)

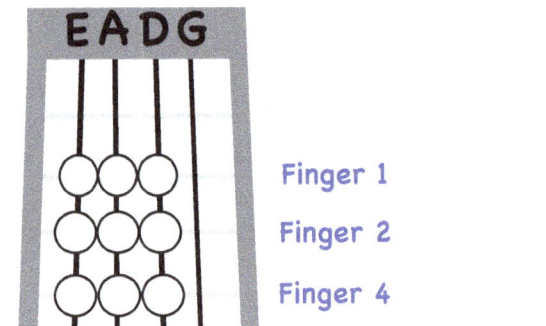
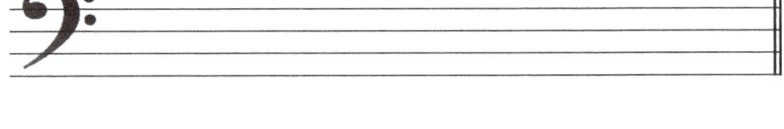

Now do the same thing on the E and C major scale. Remember to indicate where you would need to shift or pivot to and the notes which you would be shifting or pivoting on.

E major (1 octave)

C major (1 octave)

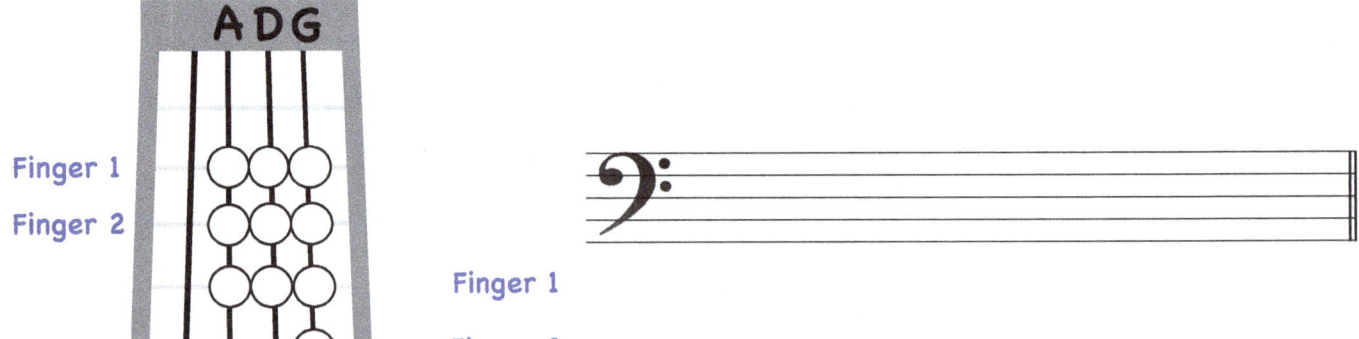

Arpeggios are notes of a chord played one after another. We mainly use the 1st, 3rd and 5th notes of a scale. We also include the 8th note.

Eg.
C Major

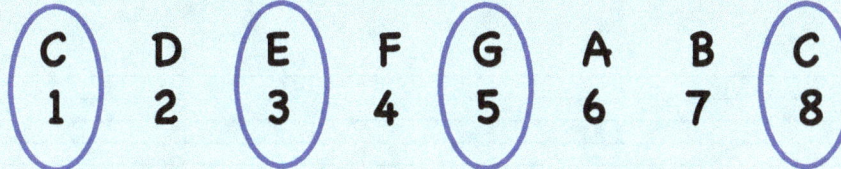

Circle the notes of the arpeggio of the scales below.

G major

        G   A   B   C   D   E   F#   G

E major

        E   F#   G#   A   B   C#   D#   E

A chord is two or more notes played together at the same time.

Using half notes, draw the notes of the arpeggio from these scales in an ascending (going up) **and descending** (going down) **order.**

 major

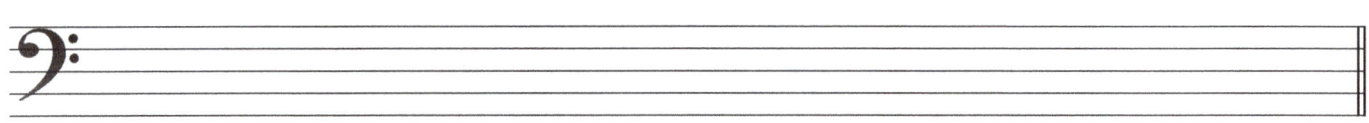

 major

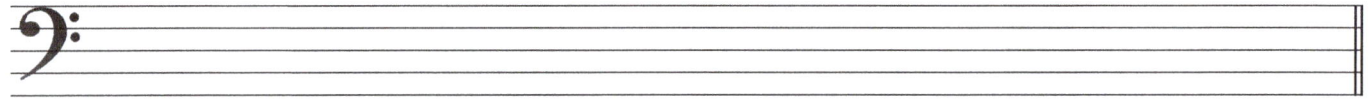

 major

Add the fingering on top of the notes and mark the notes where you would have to shift or pivot on these arpeggios.

Suzie and Tommy are learning their scales. Help Tommy find his arpeggios and Suzie find her scales.

Key Signature and Accidental

 A **key signature** tells us which notes to play with ♯s and ♭s throughout the piece. These signs are written at the beginning of each line.

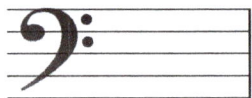

C major
There are no ♯s or ♭s in a C major scale.

G major
There is an F♯ in a G major scale.

E major
There is an F♯, C♯ and a G♯ in a E major scale.

Copy the key signature in the next 3 measures.

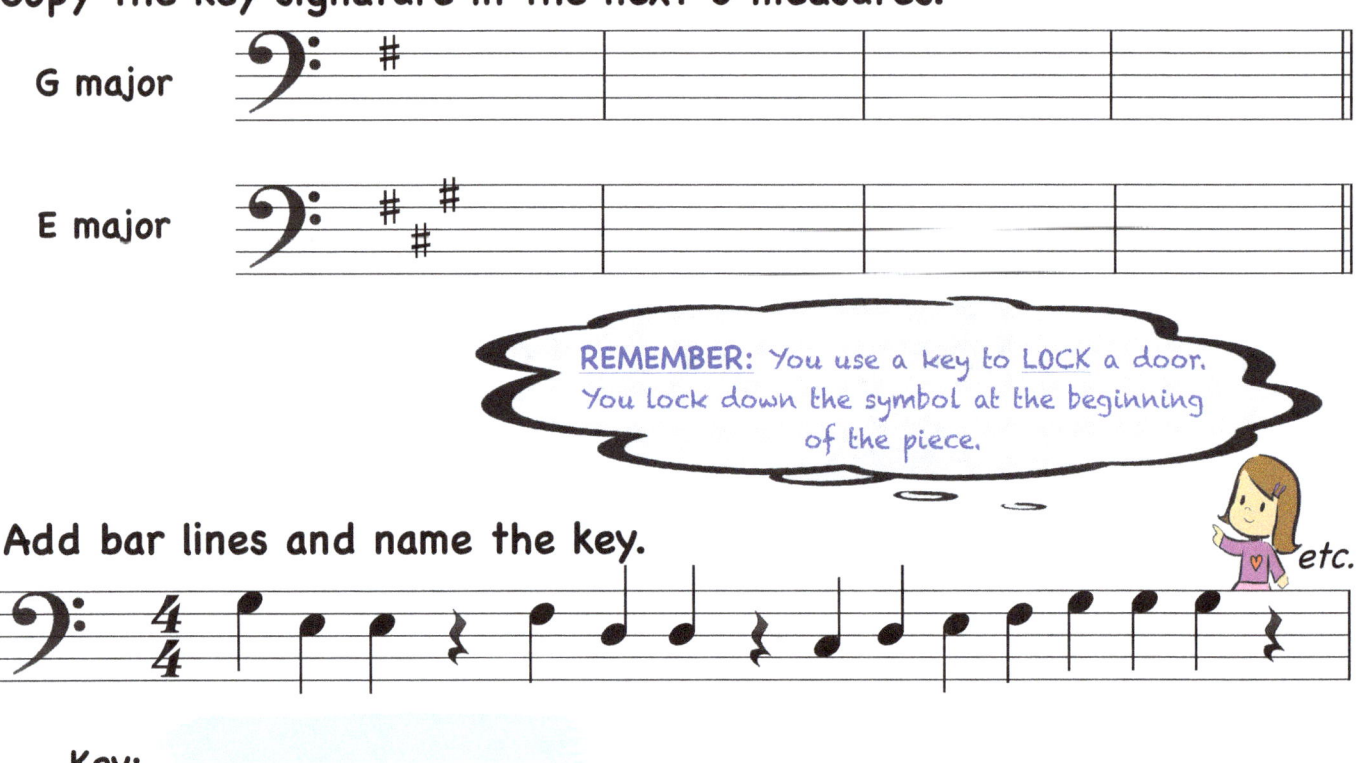

REMEMBER: You use a key to LOCK a door. You lock down the symbol at the beginning of the piece.

Add bar lines and name the key.

Key:

Key:

Key:

www.stringstastic.com   39

Accidentals are signs (♯, ♭, ♮) that are written on the left hand side of a note to change the pitch (how high or low a sound is).

Add the accidentals to the indicated keys and write in the correct time signature.

E major
*

C major
*

G major
*

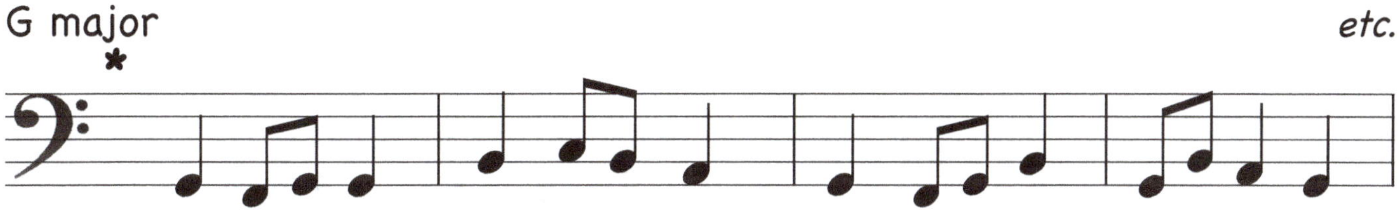

What is the difference between a key signature and an accidental?

_____

REMEMBER: Think of accidentals as an accident where a symbol is accidentally dropped next to a note.

Articulation

Articulation refers to the different ways of playing the same note creating different sounds.

On stringed instruments, articulation relies on the type of bowing or plucking technique used.

Below are a few articulations which we use as string players.

ARTICULATION	DESCRIPTION
Staccato	Short and detached (bouncy and light)
Accent / Marcato	Strong attack of a note by putting pressure on the bow when playing the note
Tenuto (legato accent)	Slight pressure placed on the bow and held for the full duration of the note
Hooked notes	2 or more notes played in the same direction of the bow with a stop between each note
slur	Playing the notes in one bow direction making the notes sound smooth and connected
pizz. (pizzicato)	Plucking the string of the instrument using your finger

Try playing each articulation on one note and using a few notes as a slur.
Did you successfully achieve this?

What are these articulations called?

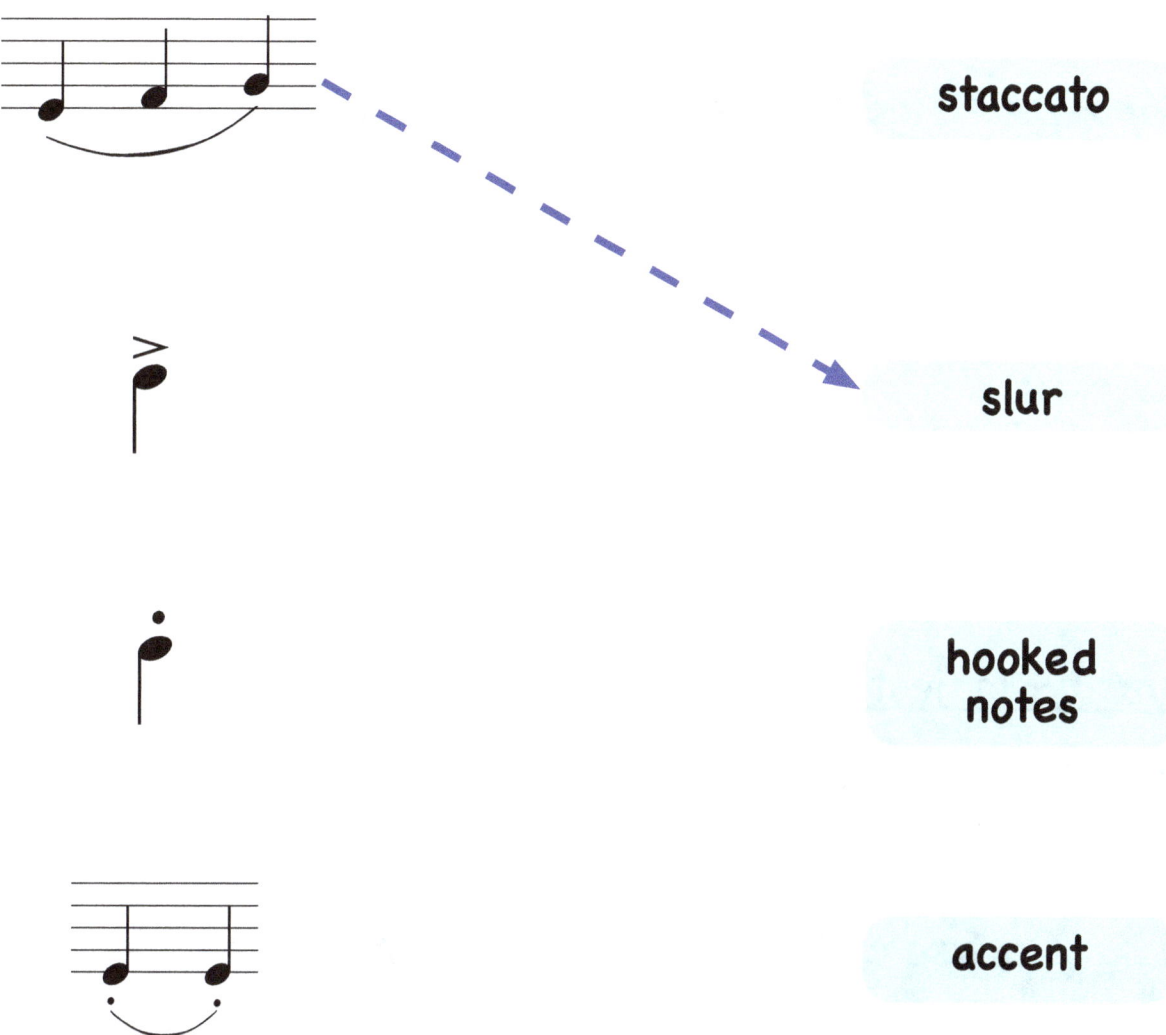

Demonstrate each articulation on the D string.

Now let us see if you can show the same articulation on a different string.

Signs

Da Capo, D.C. – go back to the beginning of the piece

Dal Segno, D.S. – go back to the sign

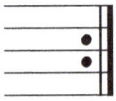 , *segno* – sign

Fine – finish

dolce – sweetly

expressivo – expressively

maestoso – majestically

con spirito – with spirit

fermata / pause – holding the note longer then its value

(Usually hold it twice as long. Think of the pause button on your TV remote control. When you press it, it freezes the video.)

REPEAT SIGNS

 – go back to the beginning and play the music again

 – play this section again

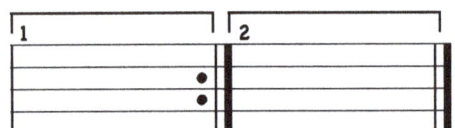 – play the 1st ending the 1st time, skip to 2nd ending on repeat

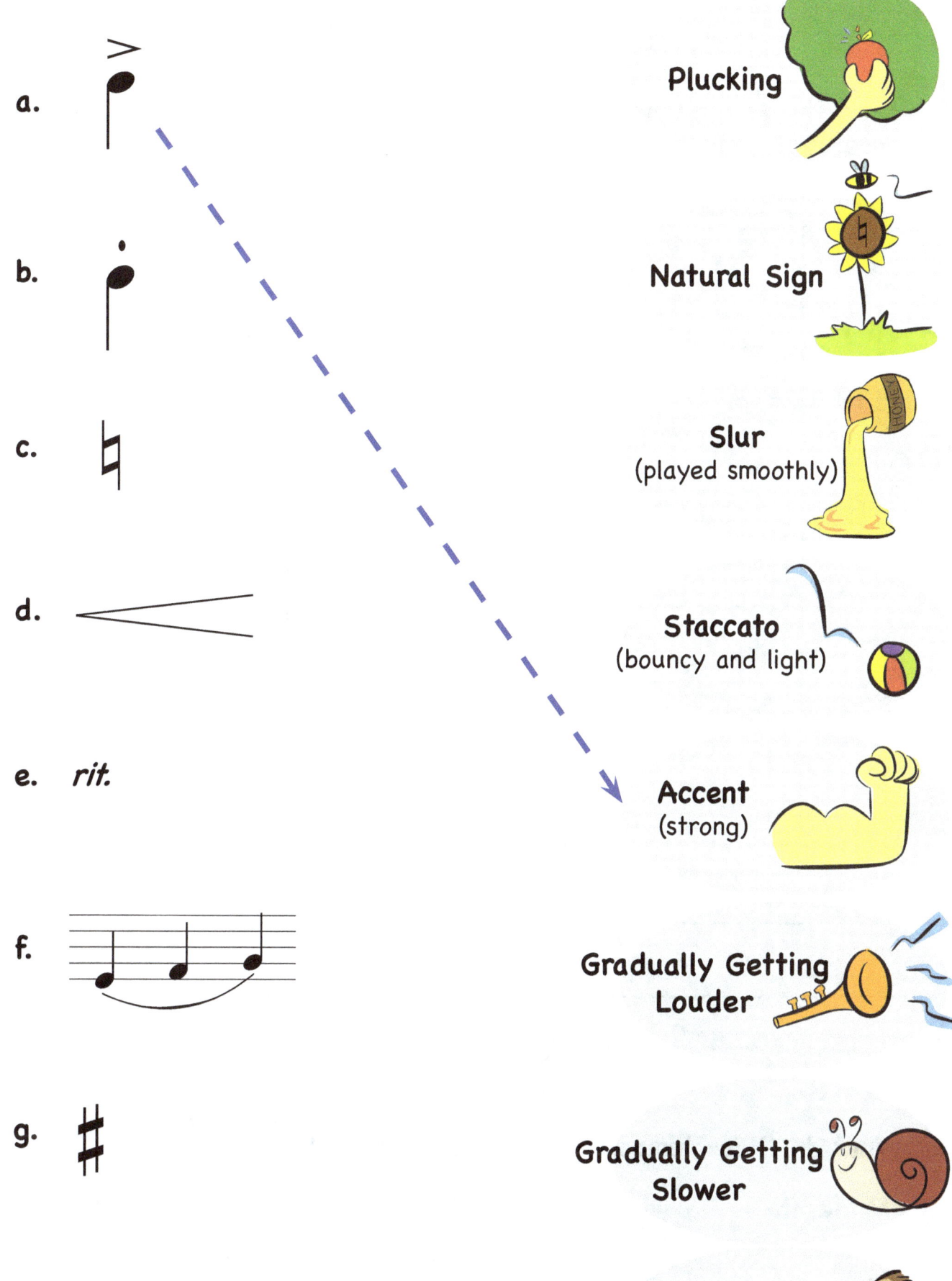

Last Revision

1. Name the string where each of these notes is from.
   (Careful of fingering.)

①③○	G	D String
①③④	F	
①③④	C	
①②④	C	
①②④	B♭	

①③	A	
①③	E	
①②④	E♭	
①③④	D	
①②④	F	

2. What is the difference between tempo and dynamics?

_____

_____

3. What do these tempo markings below mean?

a. Moderato -

b. Allegro -

c. Andante -

4. Place the correct articulation/markings to these notes and explain their meaning.

MARKINGS	ARTICULATION	MEANING
Eg. (note with > accent)	accent	*strong*
(three notes)	slur	
(two notes)	hooked notes	
(note)	sharp	
(note)	tenuto	
(note)	flat	
(note)	staccato	
(note)	natural	

5. What is the difference between key signature and accidental?

_____

_____

6. Write out these scales using the correct key signature.
   (Remember to draw the bass clef.)

   E major
   - One octave ascending only
   - Use whole notes
   - Complete the scale with a double bar line

   C major
   - One octave in an ascending and descending order
   - Use whole notes
   - Complete the scale with a double bar line

7. Write out these scales using the correct accidentals.

   G major
   - One octave descending only
   - Use whole notes
   - Complete the scale with a double bar line

8. Write out the appropriate fingering for questions 6 and 7 and play them.

www.stringstastic.com

Name: _____ Date: _____

47

Test

TOTAL MARKS: _____/100

Example 1

Christmas Song

Example 2

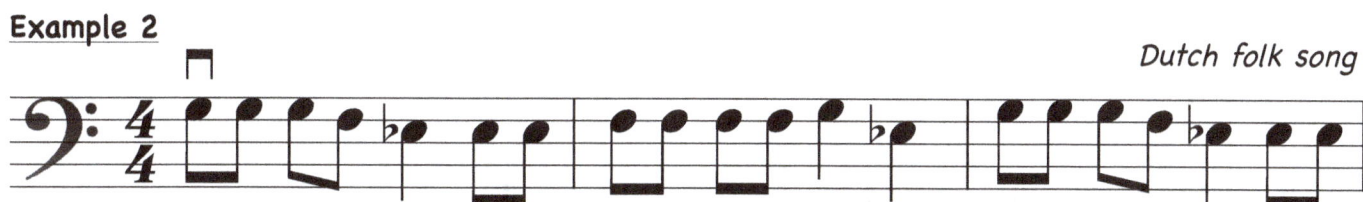

Dutch folk song

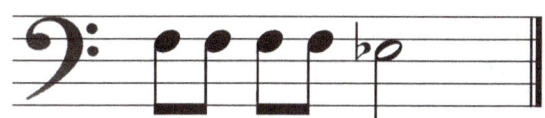

1. Write out the fingering on top of the notes to example 1 and 2.
   _____/13

2. Put a dash (-) on top of the note where shifting or pivoting occurs.
   _____/4

3. (a) Using whole notes, draw the lowest and highest notes of example 1 and 2. _____/8

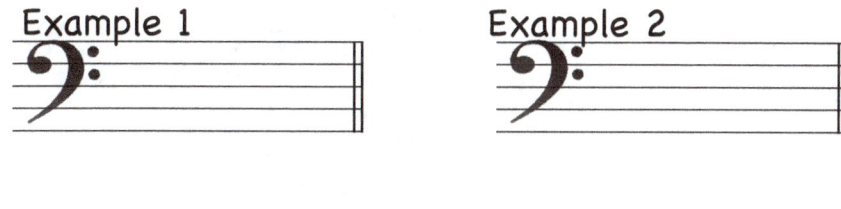

Example 1

Example 2

_____   _____

(b) Name all the notes in question 3 (a). _____/8

5. Fill in the blanks. _____/10

TERMS	DYNAMICS / TEMPO	MEANING
Eg. p	Dynamics	Soft
allegro		
andante		
<		
accel.		
mf		

6. How many spoons full of sugar should go into each drink? _____/8

7. How many times does Suzie and her friends rest before they get home? _____ /8

Robert the Chicken: _____

Cindy the Rabbit: _____

Max the Snake: _____

Suzie the Koala: _____

8. Fill in the blanks. _____ /4

	NAME THE LINE UNDER THE NOTES	HOW DO YOU PLAY THESE NOTES?

9. **Write a E major scale:** _____/5
   - Start the scale with a bass clef
   - Use accidentals
   - Use half notes
   - Write one octave on an ascending order
   - Complete the scale with a double bar line

10. **Now fill in the notes for the E major scale** (1 octave) **on the double bass fingerboard.**

   _____/8

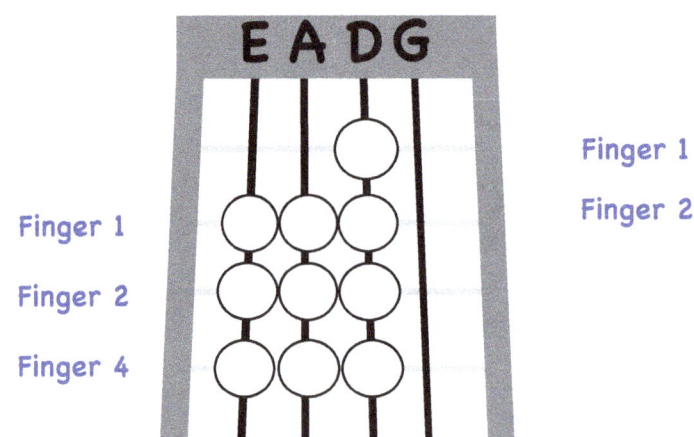

11. **There are 4 mistakes in the following G major scale. Circle them and rewrite the correct scale.** _____/14

12. Where would you be able to add a tied in the tune below?

____/2

13. Name these signs and its definition. ____/8

a.  -

b.  -

c.  -

d. 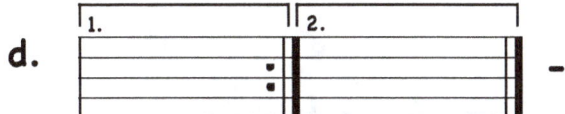 -

e. *rit.* -

f. *dolce* -

g. *Da Capo (D.C.)* -

h. *Fine* -

www.ingramcontent.com/pod-product-compliance
Lightning Source LLC
Chambersburg PA
CBHW080856010526
44107CB00057B/2596